LET'S MAKE A KITE!

BY JACK STOKES

HENRY Z. WALCK, INC. • NEW YORK

Copyright © 1976 by Jack Stokes. All rights reserved. ISBN: 0-679-20325-7 LC: 75-35476
Printed in the United States of America. Cataloging in Publication Data can be found on the last page.

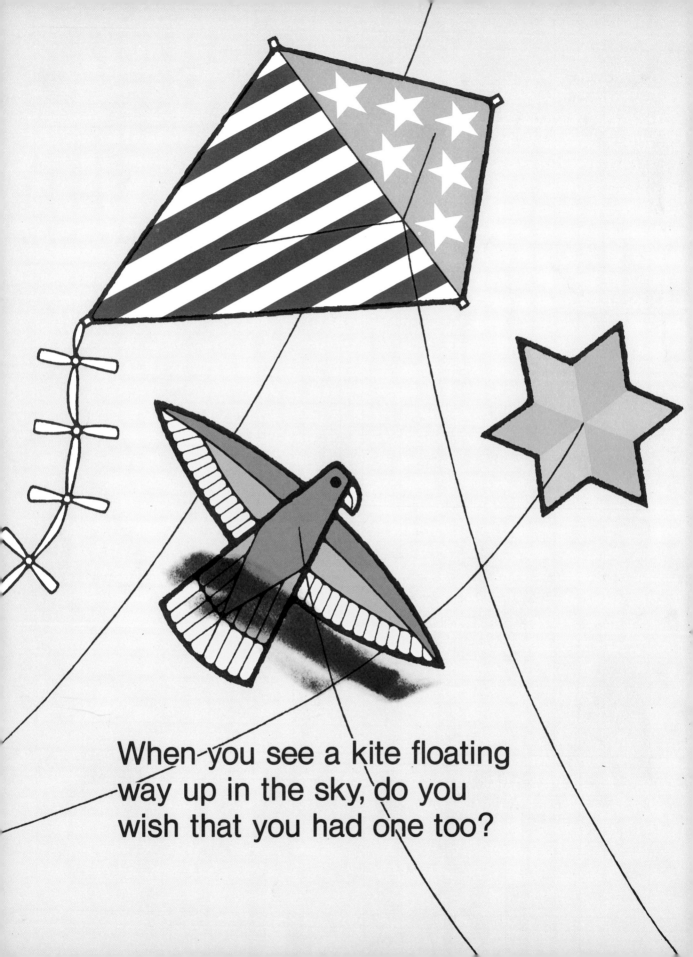

When you see a kite floating
way up in the sky, do you
wish that you had one too?

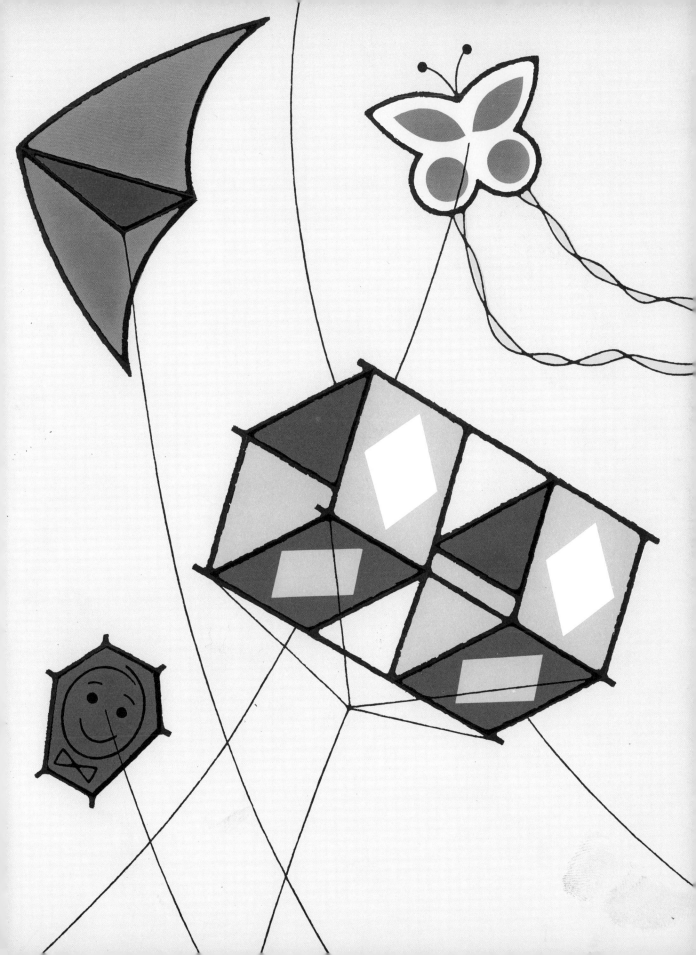

You can make your own kite,
something that flies and is yours.
It can look very special
and it's fun to do.

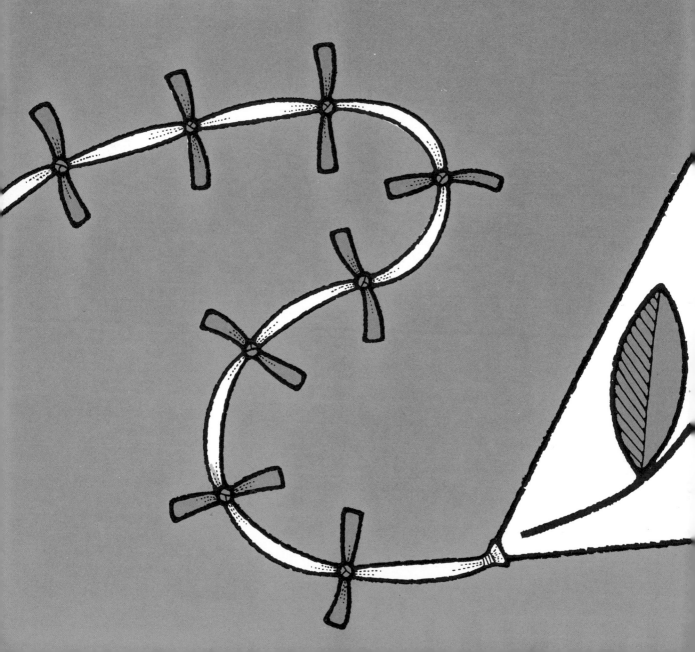

First you need
two long lightweight sticks.
Use strips from ...

old window shades

bamboo blinds

wooden moldings

or buy
carpenter's dowels
about as thick
as a pencil.

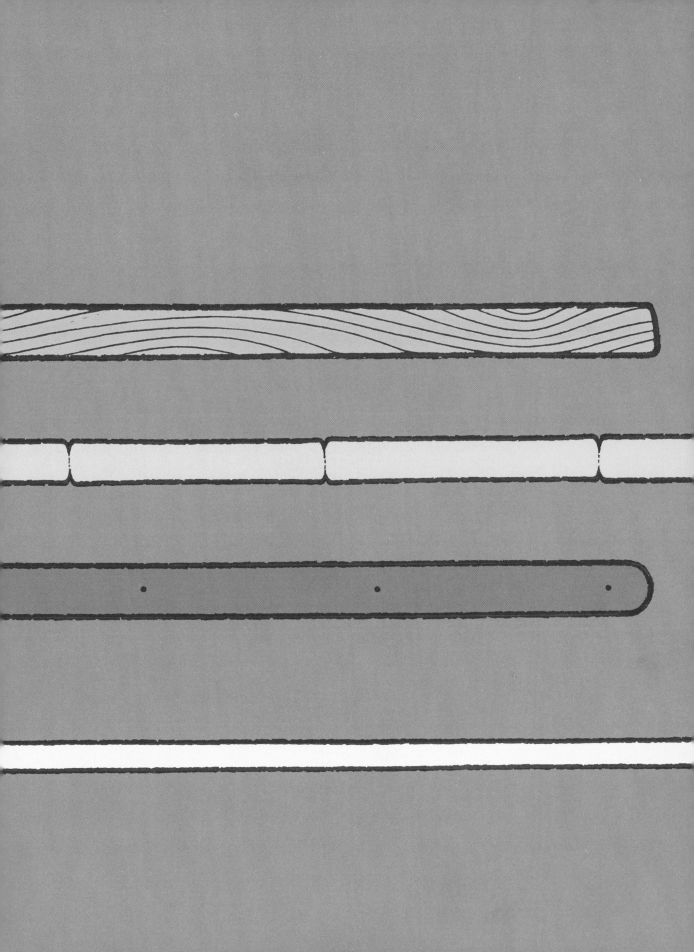

The up and down stick
is called a spine.
You can cut it
30 inches long
for this kite.

The cross stick
is called a spar.
Make it
24 inches long.

If you use the
metric system,
there are substitute
measurements
on the last page
of this book.

Ask a grown-up
to help you saw
or cut a slit
in both ends
of each stick.

Or you can
file notches.

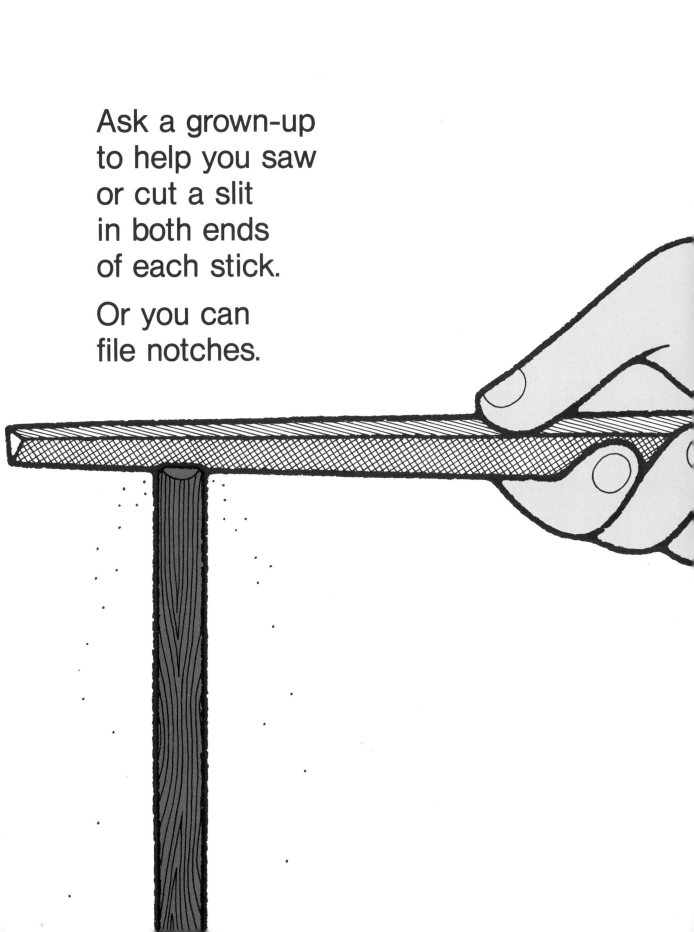

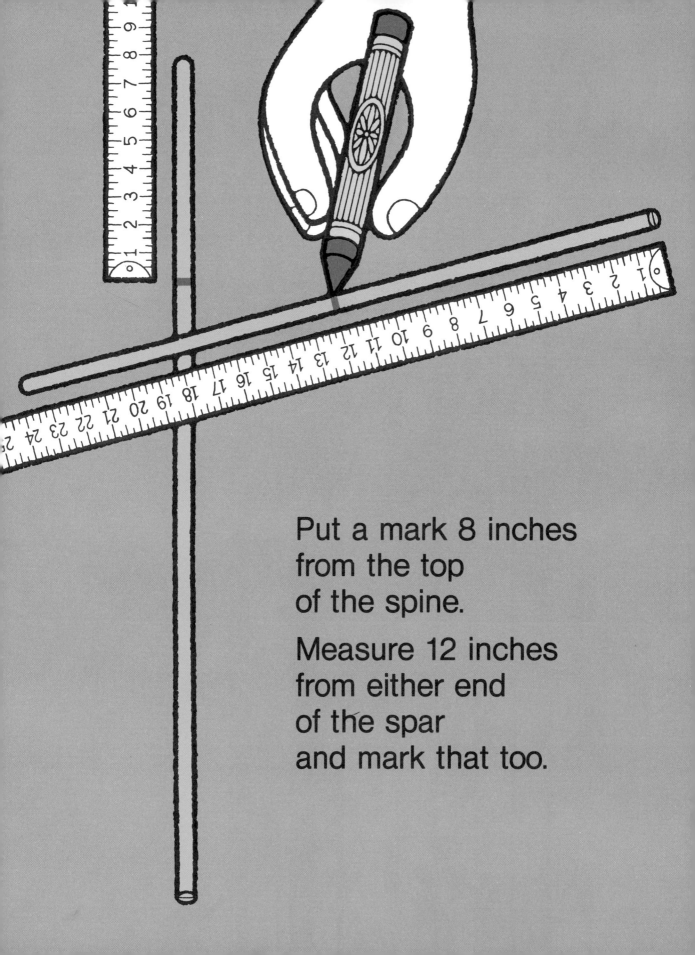

Put a mark 8 inches
from the top
of the spine.

Measure 12 inches
from either end
of the spar
and mark that too.

Cross the spine
and the spar
on these marks.

Then tie and
glue the sticks
together.

You can use
this book to
line them up.

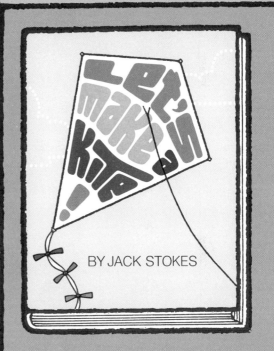

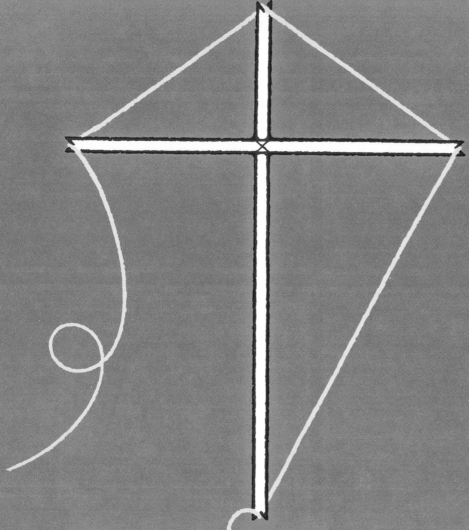

After the glue dries, run a string
snugly around the notches.

This makes a frame
for the paper covering.

Tie and knot both ends of the string
at the bottom.

Leave a few inches hanging down
to attach a tail when it is ready.

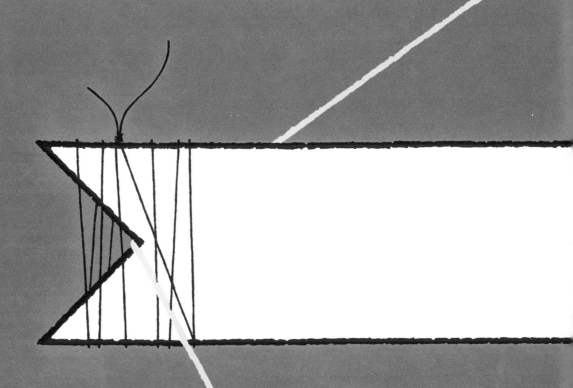

With some strong thread wrap a few
turns at the bottom of each notch.

This will stop the wood
from splitting.

Then make a few more turns at the
end of each stick and knot tightly.

This will keep the string
from slipping loose.

Sticky tape may be used
in place of thread.

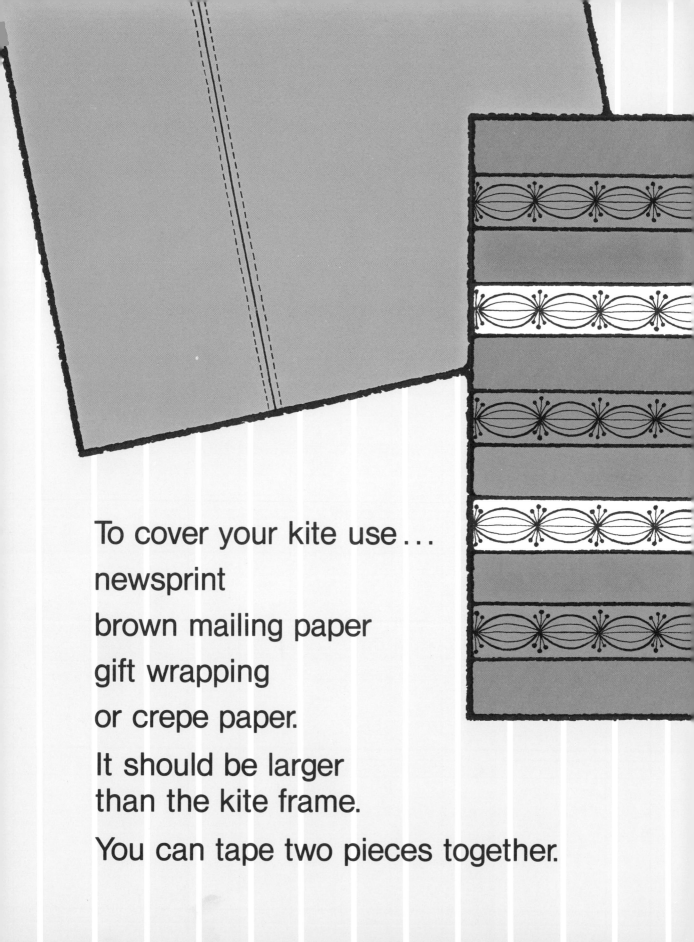

To cover your kite use ...

newsprint

brown mailing paper

gift wrapping

or crepe paper.

It should be larger
than the kite frame.

You can tape two pieces together.

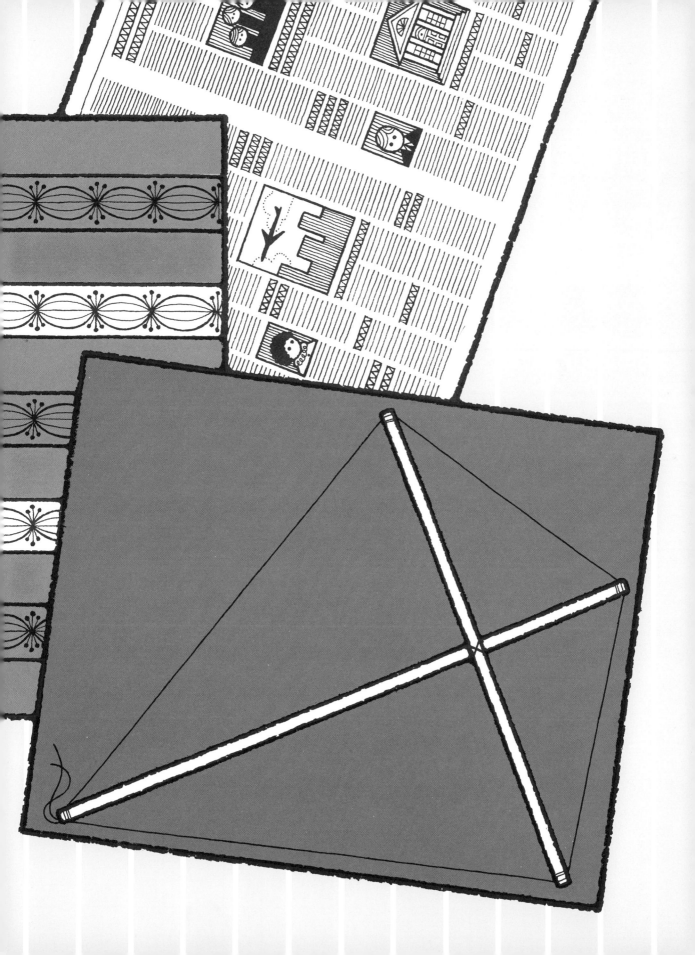

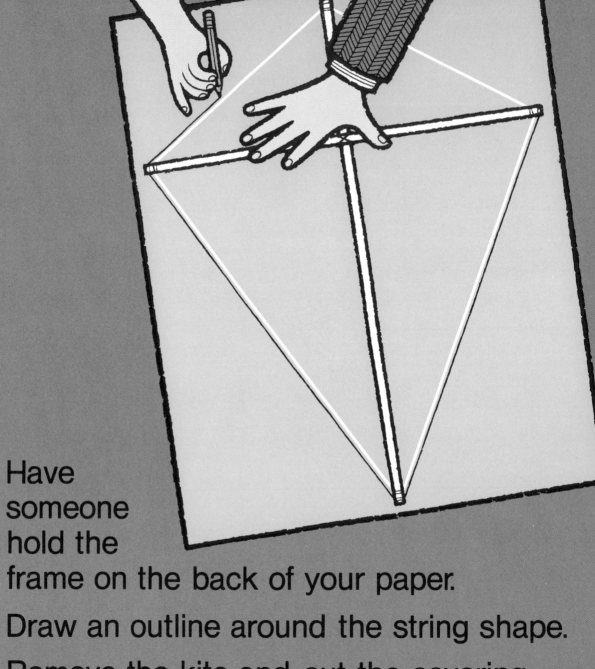

Have
someone
hold the
frame on the back of your paper.

Draw an outline around the string shape.

Remove the kite and cut the covering
about an inch larger than this outline.

Snip off the corners of the paper.

With the spine facing down, fold the
paper over the string.

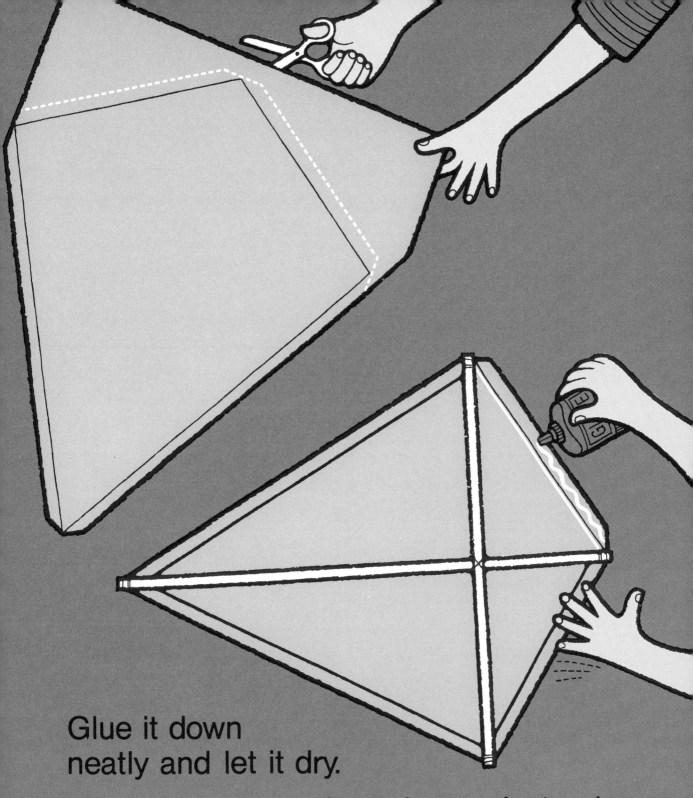

Glue it down
neatly and let it dry.

You may use see-through tape instead
of glue if you press it down firmly.

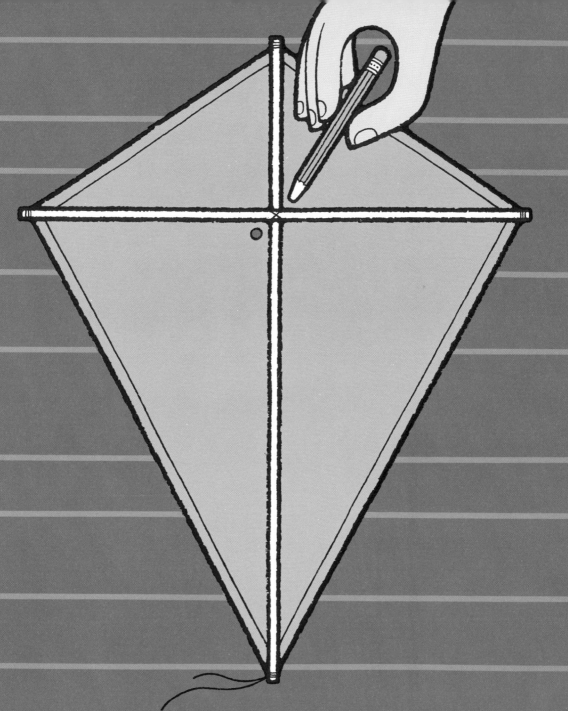

From the back of your kite punch two small holes with a pencil.

Later you will run a flying line through these holes to tie it to the frame.

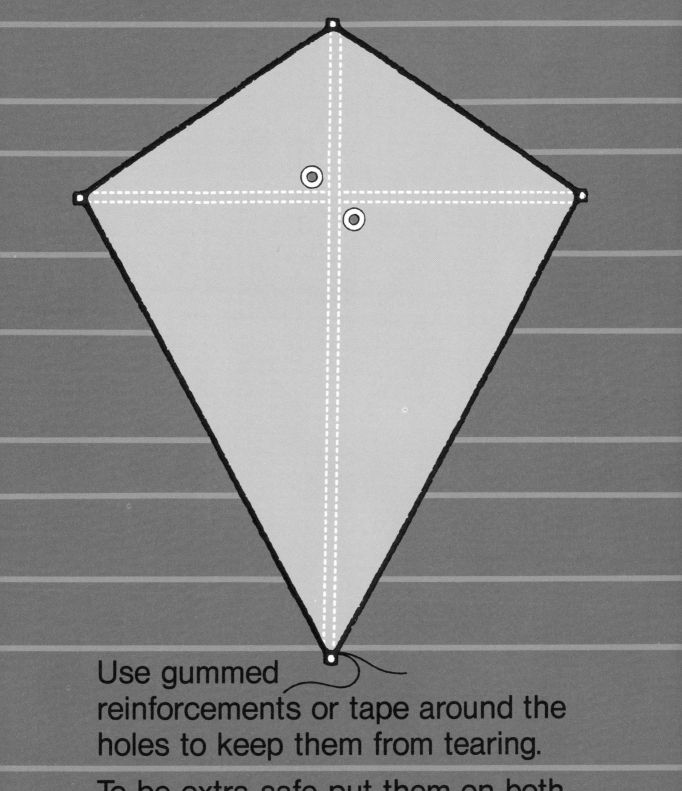

Use gummed reinforcements or tape around the holes to keep them from tearing.

To be extra safe put them on both the front and back of the kite.

Now you can paint the front of
your kite just the way you want to.

Draw airplanes, faces, ships,
birds, fish, your initials
or anything at all.

Make it big and bright
so your kite will show up when
it's flying high overhead.

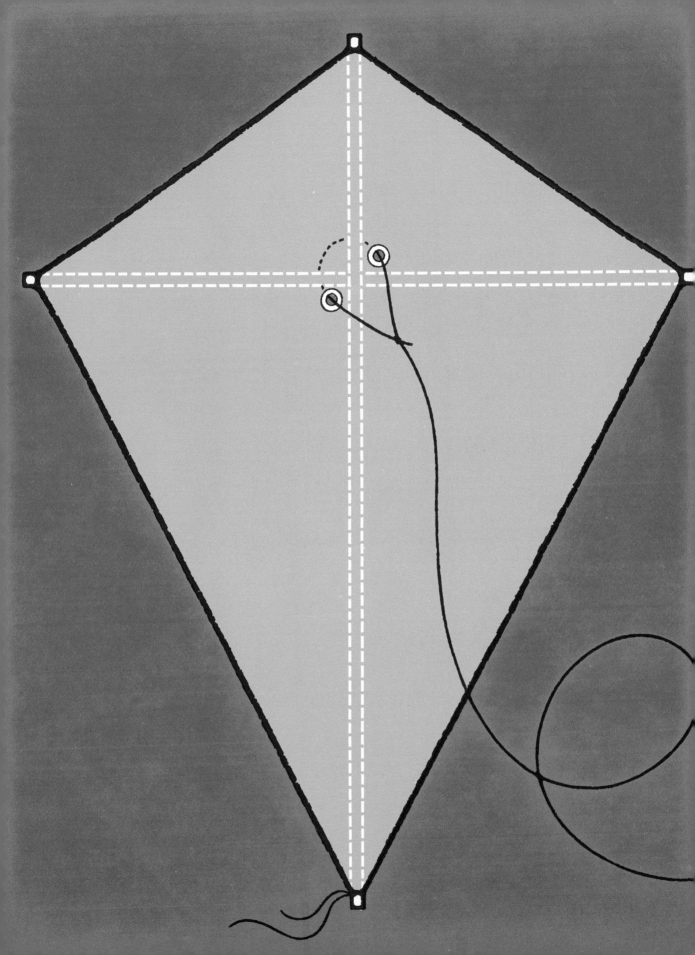

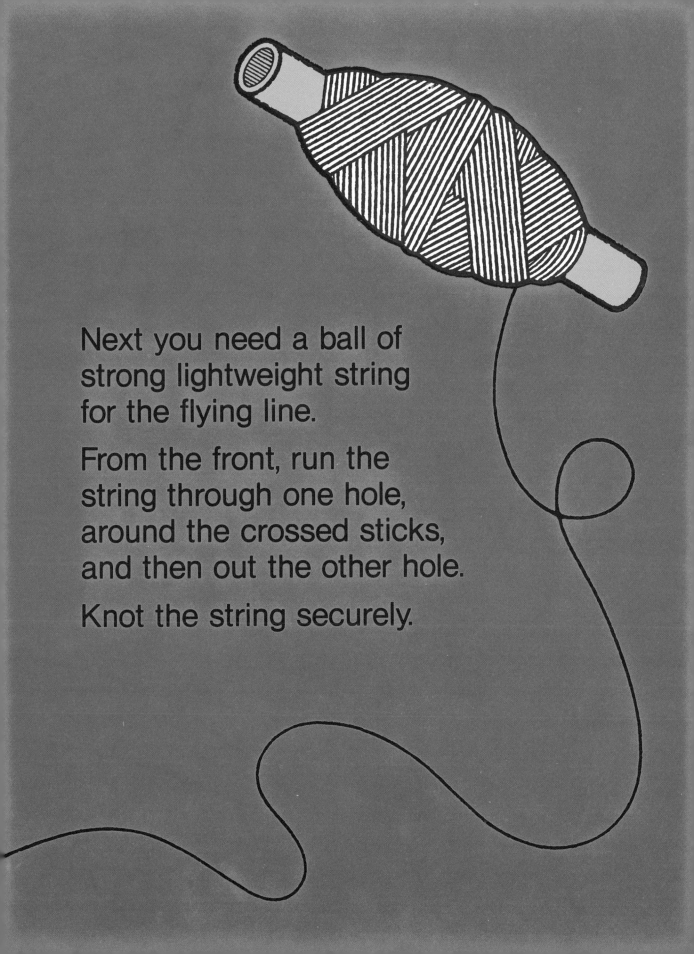

Next you need a ball of
strong lightweight string
for the flying line.

From the front, run the
string through one hole,
around the crossed sticks,
and then out the other hole.

Knot the string securely.

To make a tail use old cotton sheets, curtains, dresses or shirts.

Cut or tear long strips 2 inches wide.

Tie them together until the tail is 13 feet long.

Cut the rest of your strips into pieces 12 inches long. Use lots of colors if you like.

Tie one of these pieces in a bow about every foot on the tail. Use a double knot.

When you are finished, attach this tail to the piece of string you left hanging at the bottom of your kite.

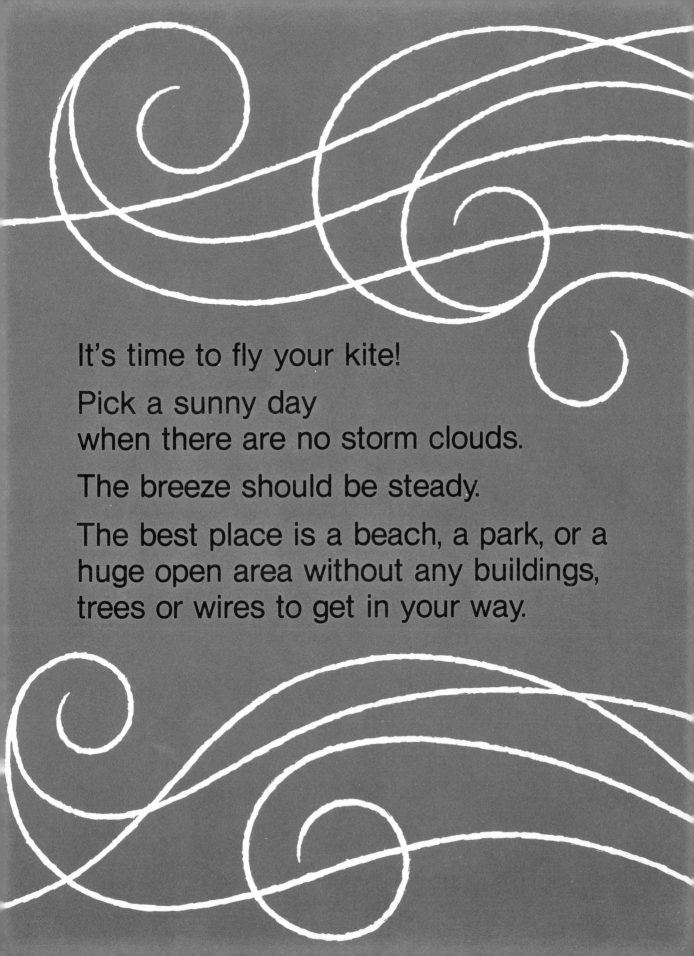

It's time to fly your kite!

Pick a sunny day
when there are no storm clouds.

The breeze should be steady.

The best place is a beach, a park, or a
huge open area without any buildings,
trees or wires to get in your way.

Stand with your back to the wind.

Get a friend to stand away from you, holding the kite with the paper side toward the wind and the tail stretched out straight.

When the breeze pushes on the kite your helper can toss it up.

Let out the string as fast as your kite will take it. Sometimes running into the wind helps too.

You will soon get the feel of the gentle pull on the string when everything is right.

It's a wonderful feeling
to watch a kite
that you made
sail up in the air.

With a little luck
it will stay there.

Wind in the string
when you want
to bring the kite down.

Then you are ready
to fly it again
and again and again....

If you use the metric system, follow these approximate measurements to build your kite.

30 inches.....75 centimeters
24 inches.....60 centimeters
8 inches.....20 centimeters
12 inches.....30 centimeters
(1 foot)
2 inches.....5 centimeters
13 feet.....4 meters

Library of Congress Cataloging in Publication Data
Stokes, Jack.
Let's make a kite!
SUMMARY: Directions for making and flying a
simple kite.
1. Kites—Juvenile literature. [1. Kites]
I. Title.
TL759.5.S77   745.59'2   75-35476
ISBN 0-679-20325-7